Harmony Loves to Ask Why

By

Teesjah & Harmony Brown

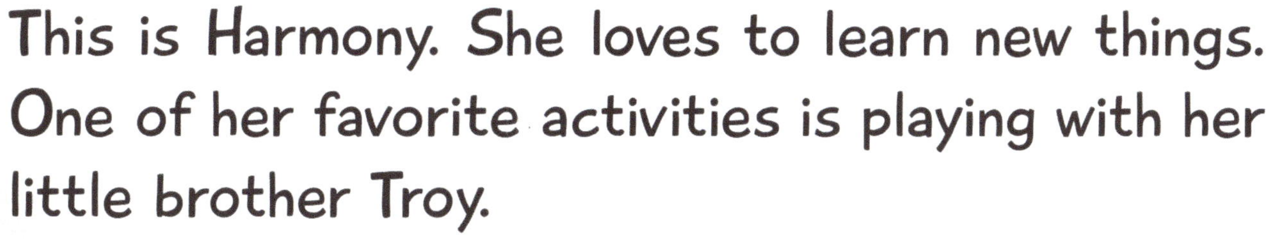

This is Harmony. She loves to learn new things. One of her favorite activities is playing with her little brother Troy.

She also loves to help her mommy and daddy whenever she can.
She also loves asking why. Do you want to know why? That's because she's curious about everything!

One day, Harmony's mommy came looking for her. "Harmony, can you please clean your play area?" her mommy asked.

"Why, Mommy?" asked Harmony, "Why do I have to clean the play area?"
"It is always a good idea to clean up after playing," said her mommy, "That way, it can be clean for the next time."

"Oh, I see!" said Harmony. So, she cleaned up her play area like her mommy told her to do.

After that, Harmony sat down on the floor with her coloring book. After coloring a picture, she stood up with excitement and ran into the next room!

Crayon
Crayon
Crayon

With her picture in hand, she left her markers behind on the floor.
She was looking for Troy when she heard her mommy.

COLORING
BOOK
Crayon
Crayon
Crayon
Crayon
Crayon
Crayon
Crayon

Crayon
Crayon
Crayon
Crayon
Crayon

"Harmony! Where are you?" her mommy asked, "You must get your Markers off the floor, please!"
"Why, mommy?" Harmony asked, "Why do I have to pick them up?"

"You must put your markers away so that Troy can't grab them," said her mommy, "It will help keep him safe since he is still a baby."

Harmony nodded. "What if Troy puts those markers in his mouth?" asked her mommy, "Or, Daddy may rush through the room and slip on them!"

Crayon
Crayon
Crayon
Crayon

Crayon
Crayon
Crayon
Crayon
Crayon
Crayon

"That would be terrible!" said Harmony.
And so, she picked up the markers from the floor
and put them into her markers box. "Good girl!" said
her mommy.

After dinner, everyone went to wash up. Harmony wanted to give her dolly a bath as well because she was dirty.

"Mommy, can I give my dolly a bath?" she asked.
"I think it would be best if I help you with that."
said her mommy.

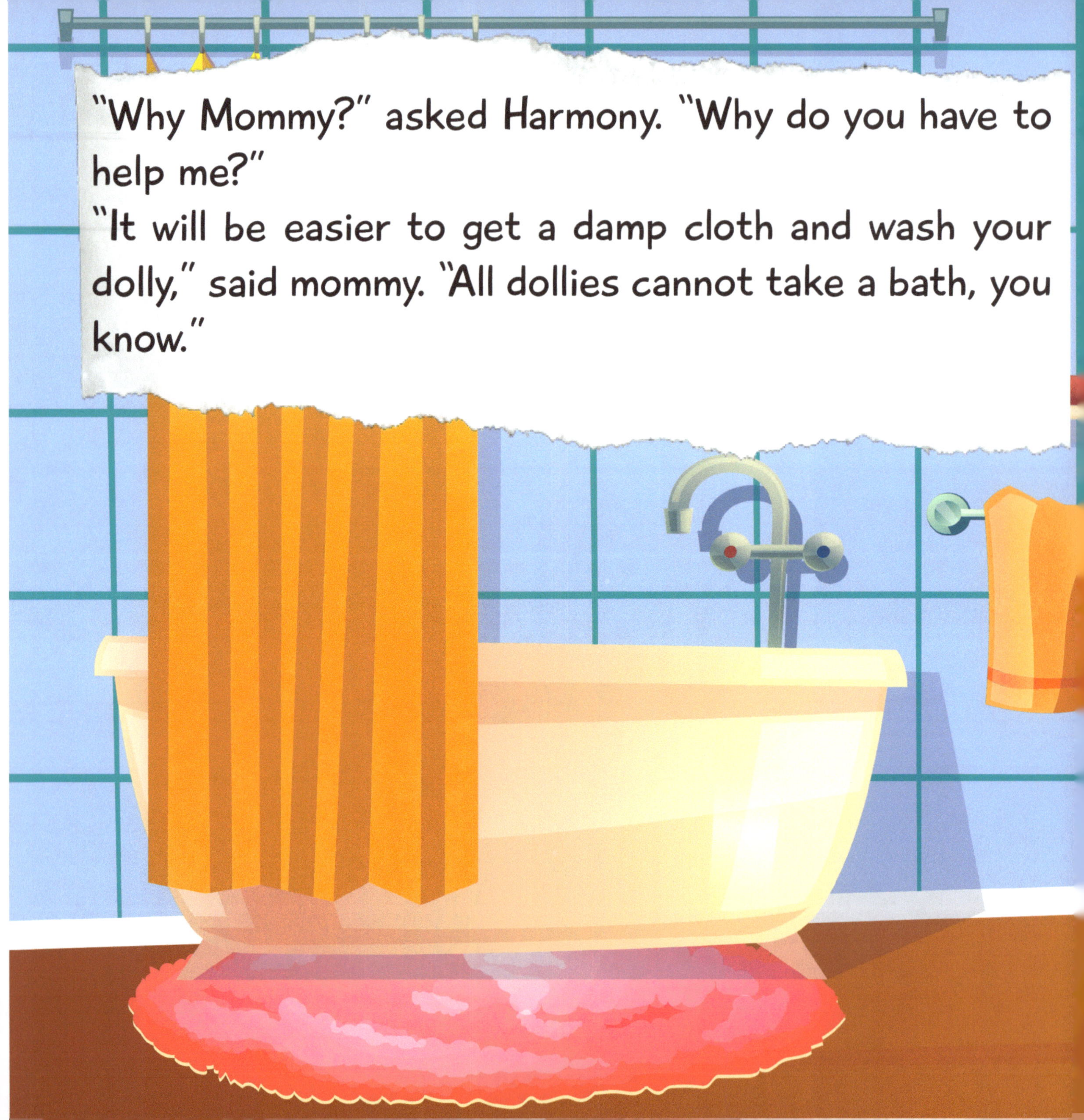

"Why Mommy?" asked Harmony. "Why do you have to help me?"
"It will be easier to get a damp cloth and wash your dolly," said mommy. "All dollies cannot take a bath, you know."

"Oh," said Harmony.
While they were bathing the dolly, her mommy said something very interesting.

"When Mommy asks you to do something, you don't always have to ask why,". "Sometimes you can think about it and tell me why."

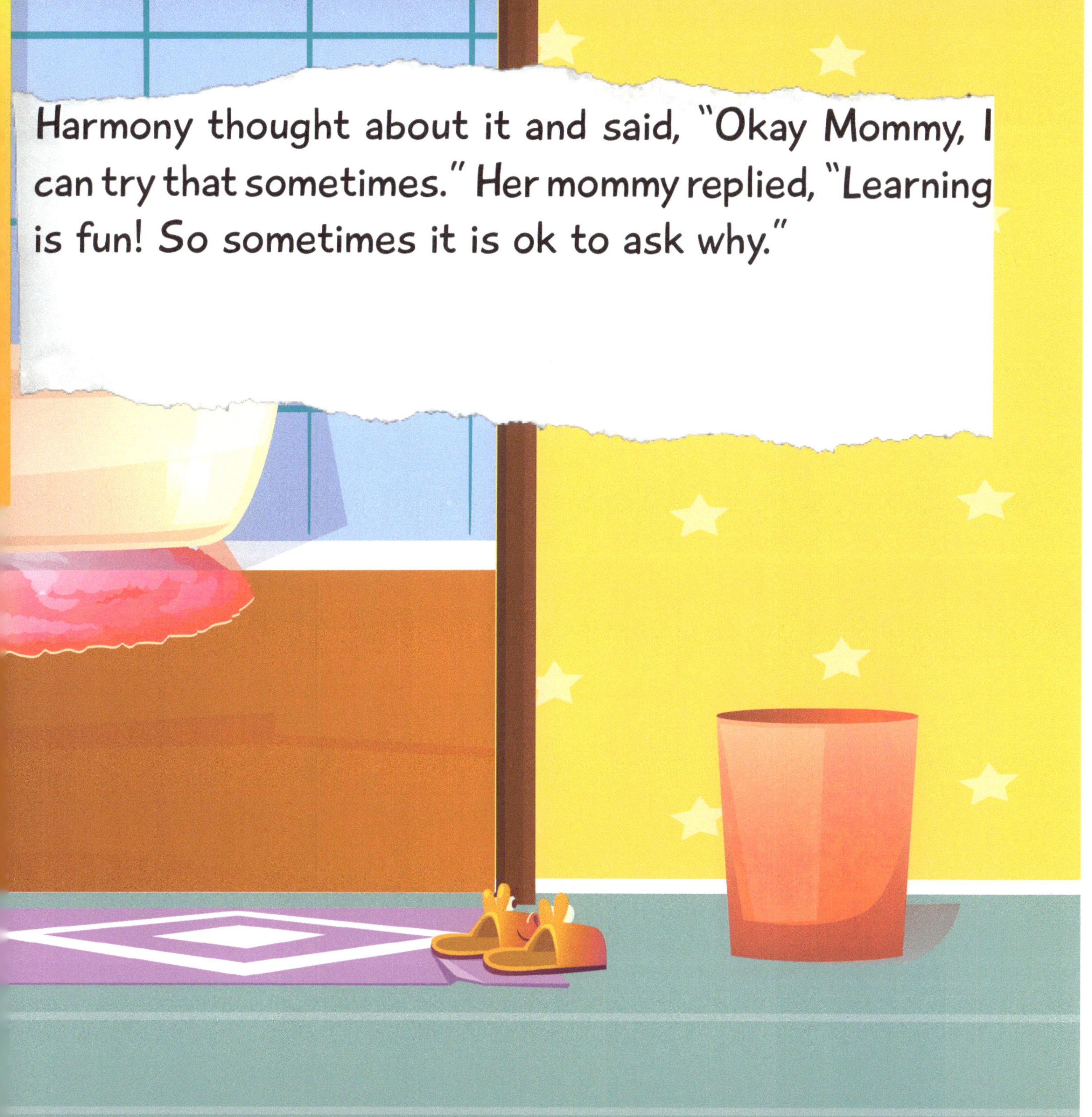

Harmony thought about it and said, "Okay Mommy, I can try that sometimes." Her mommy replied, "Learning is fun! So sometimes it is ok to ask why."

"You're right!. "Learning is fun!" said Harmony with a smile.
After bathing her dolly, Harmony was ready for sleep. She laid in her bed as her mommy tucked her in and gave her a kiss on the forehead.

"Go to sleep, Sweetie..." said her mommy.
Harmony wanted to ask why, but she remembered what her mommy said. So, she thought about why she had to sleep.

"I have to sleep so that I have plenty of energy tomorrow!" she said, "That's why!"
And so, she fell asleep with a smile on her face.

The End

www.ingramcontent.com/pod-product-compliance
Lightning Source LLC
Chambersburg PA
CBHW041645110726